DRIED & PRESSED
FLOWERS

A Beginner's Guide to Floral Arrangements

Contributing Writer: Kathy Lamancusa
Floral Designer and Contributing Writer: Maria J. Buscemi

Publications International, Ltd.

•Cont

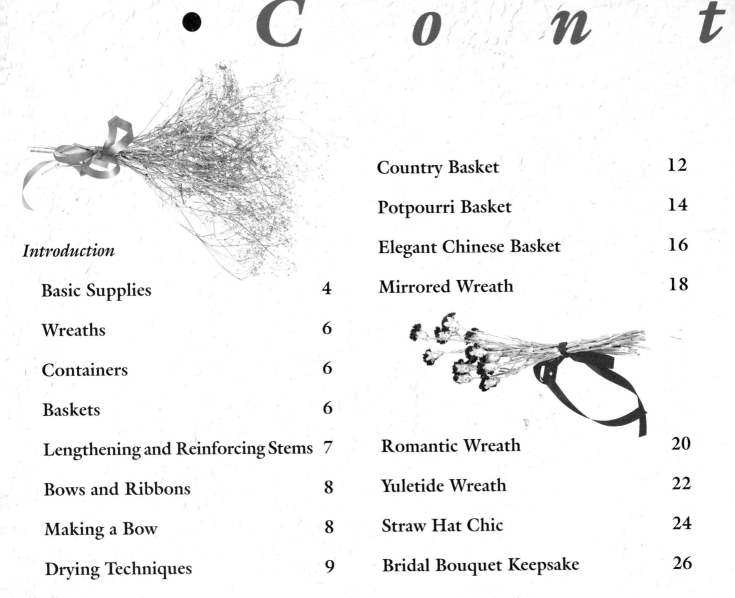

Introduction

Louis Weber, C.E.O.
Publications International, Ltd.
7373 North Cicero Avenue
Lincolnwood, Illinois 60646

Permission is never granted for commercial purposes.

Manufactured in the U.S.A.

8 7 6 5 4 3 2 1

ISBN 1-56173-290-7

Floral Designer and Contributing Writer: Maria J. Buscemi

Maria Buscemi is a floral design instructor at the Cooking and Hospitality Institute of Chicago.

Projects Coordinator: Don Newcomb

Don Newcomb is Chairman of the Horticulture Department at Triton College, where he teaches classes in floral design, manages the botanic garden and greenhouses, and sponsors frequent flower shows.

ents

Contributing Writer: Kathy Lamancusa

Kathy Lamancusa is the author of over 20 books and many magazine articles on dried flower arrangements. When not involved in writing and designing, Kathy and her husband present on-stage educational shows for businesses in the floral and craft industries. She is currently vice president of Visual Design Concepts.

Model: Pam Kaplanes/Royal Model Management

All photography by Siede/Preis Photography and Sam Griffith Studios.

Contac® is a registered trademark of Rubbermaid Incorporated. Styrofoam® is a registered trademark of Dow Chemical Company.

Introduction

Flowers are a part of our lives and our heritage. They have a calming effect on us as we walk through a garden filled with colors, scents, and textures. For centuries, our ancestors appreciated flowers and decorated their homes with both fresh and dried varieties. They called the dried flowers "everlastings," since their beauty could be enjoyed even in the dead of winter. Our ancestors loved to be surrounded with flowers all year long, and they developed the methods by which this desire was made a reality.

Flowers have always enjoyed a place of honor in our lives and our hearts, since they are often the main focus in many of our most joyous and memorable occasions. They express both sad and happy feelings. Flowers also set the scene and speak to us during special times of our lives that evoke joy, congratulations, or sympathy.

Designing with dried flowers is an art that is easily learned, but it does entail quite a bit of trial and error. We hope this book will put you on the road to success. It will take you through all the basics you need to know to get started. It will also get you started on several easy projects, explained in a way that you will have no trouble following. Use your imagination and the information you learn to expand and create your own designs.

Basic Supplies

You will need several tools and supplies to get started creating arrangements with dried and pressed flowers. These items can be purchased at local floral, craft, or hardware stores.

1. *Wire cutters* are necessary when cutting the wires attached, or being attached, to flowers. Two weights, heavy and light, are recommended.

2. *Floral knife* cuts flower stems and splits flower parts for various arranging techniques.

3. *Stem wire* reinforces or creates a new stem on dried flowers. Many gauges, or thicknesses, of wire are available. The larger the number, the thinner the wire is. Either 28 or 30 gauge is the best for floral purposes.

4. *Spool wire* is available in fine, medium, and heavy sizes. This wire is used for garlands and wreaths, as well as for winding around floral heads when rewiring.

5. *Floral tape* is useful for attaching wires to flower stems. It is not a sticky tape and will only stick to itself when it has been stretched and wound around a floral stem. In addition to green, it is also available in brown, white, and selected designer colors for specialty uses.

6. *Wired wood picks* are effective when used for lengthening or reinforcing stems. They provide a firm stem base for insertion into foam when the existing stem is weak.

7. *Greening pins* are U-shaped pins that are also called *pole pins* and *craft pins*. They are excellent for securing items. When attaching moss, simply insert the pin through the moss and into the foam. Greening pins can also be placed over stems of dried materials and inserted into foam or wreath bases.

8. *Dry floral foam* is usually deep brown in color. Dried and preserved flowers should always be inserted into dry floral foam for stability. This foam is purchased in blocks and can be cut to any size with a serrated knife. It is usually attached to a container with hot glue or craft glue. Dry foam can also be wired in place in baskets. (Do not confuse this product with wet floral foam that is normally green. Wet foam is strictly used for fresh flowers. It is soaked in water, and fresh flowers are inserted into the wet foam so they can draw up moisture.)

9. *Scissors* have endless uses, since they are handy for everything from cutting ribbon to trimming leaves and stems.

10. *Wire snips* are used for cutting very heavy wire stems or thick lengths of wire. Wire snips are stronger than normal wire cutters, making them ideal for cutting wire frames and forms.

11. *Hot glue gun* is a tool that a floral designer should not be without. Hot glue dries very quickly and is the desired method for gluing dried materials and arrangements. Just be careful when applying the glue, since it is very HOT. If your glue gun

does not have a stand, find a piece of cardboard or an old plate to place the nozzle on when working. It is important for the life span of the hot glue gun to keep it in an upright position as you work. Do not let it remain on its side for a longer period of time than necessary.

Larger items may need to be held in place for a minute or two before the glue has a chance to dry. In some cases, the items should be wired on first, then reinforced with glue. You may notice strings extending from your work to the gun. Do not be alarmed—this is merely the glue cooling quickly. Simply pull the strings off your work. If the dried flowers you are working with are not extremely fragile, a blow dryer works well to melt the strings of glue and make them disappear.

Apply the glue to the flower stems rather than to the petals to keep from scorching the flowers. Keep a bowl of ice water near your work area for potential burns, and never allow an unattended child near a hot glue gun.

12. *Craft glue* is water-based glue that is useful for reattaching petals that have fallen off. It is also good background adhesive for pressed flower work.

13. *Tweezers,* in either metal or plastic, are useful for moving flowers and greens when pressing.

14. *Tape measure* is useful when measurements need to be taken for establishing the sizes for floral designs or dimensions of pressed flower work.

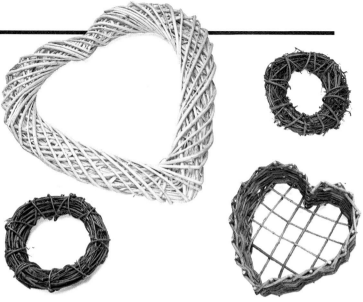

Wreaths

Wreath backgrounds are favorites for creating dried floral designs. A huge variety is available in the marketplace with new choices being released yearly. When choosing a wreath base, decide the mood and feeling you wish to convey with the design; then consider the types of dried flowers you will be working with. Size is important as well. Larger dried flowers should be placed on a larger wreath form. Small, delicate materials will find a better home on a smaller, more delicate wreath base.

Containers

The container you choose should complement the style of the design you wish to create. It should not stand out on its own, but rather become a secondary feature to the completed design. Choose containers that coordinate in color and style with the flowers you have decided to use. The container need not be expensive. Begin creating your own "container library" by shopping at garage sales, flea markets, and closeout sales at your local variety, floral, or craft shop. Remember —containers are reusable—so don't throw away your favorites.

Baskets

A basket is a good choice as the container for a dried flower arrangement. Baskets are reasonably priced and there is no end to the shapes, sizes, unusual textures, and fiber combinations available.

In some cases, baskets may present a problem. A tall basket, for example, will need some sort of weight in the base to keep it from toppling over. Simply place a large, flat stone, brick, bag of pebbles, or sand into the bottom of the basket before putting the foam inside. Other baskets may be slightly off balance due to travel and being solidly packed in cartons. Always check how the basket sits on a flat surface before purchasing it. Often, it can simply be pushed back into shape. However, if it does not stay, be careful. It may be difficult to work with and probably impossible to design correctly.

Check the basket for uneven wicker ends that may snag or detract from the finished design. Be sure the handle is securely attached and will not loosen in time. If you purchase a basket that is off balance, hold it over a pot of steaming water for a minimum of five minutes or until you feel the fibers softening. Place it on a flat surface to reshape. Hold it in place with a heavy weight until the fibers dry and become firm again. If they do not respond, repeat the entire process, steaming for a longer period of time until the basket stays as you want it.

Lengthening and Reinforcing Stems

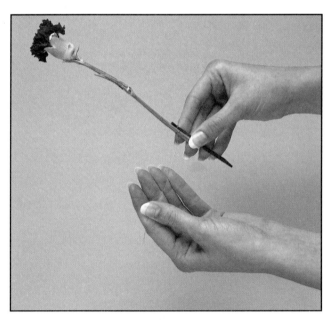

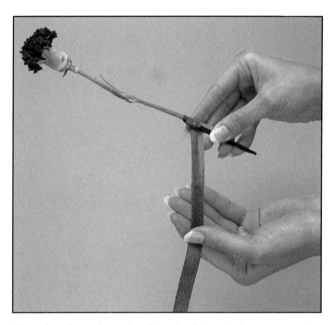

Often when a flower dries, its stem becomes brittle. Be careful when you insert these flowers into floral foam. It is advisable to reinforce the stem end with a wood pick. Since wood picks are available in many lengths, they are an excellent way to lengthen the stem to the desired measurement when creating a floral design.

Simply place the wired end of the pick next to the flower stem overlapping approximately ½ to 1 inch. Wind the wire snugly around the stem. If desired, the reinforced stem can also be floral-taped to further secure the pick to the stem and to eliminate any chance of the flower slipping in the design.

Bows are beautiful accents to any dried or pressed flower design. And with today's large selection on the market, you can always find something appropriate. Some ribbons are elegant; others are more casual. Always choose bows that work well with the flowers and container being used.

Size also plays an important role in the overall planning of the floral design. Narrow ribbons will not be as prominent as wider ones. You can also combine several ribbon widths together in a bow to add additional texture and interest. Be aware of the visual weight each style of ribbon will add. Wider, solid ribbons will appear larger and fuller than narrower, lacy patterns. This is an important element to remember when deciding whether you want the ribbons or the flowers to play a more important role in the visual look of the finished design.

Materials such as raffia or handmade paper can also be used in bowlike treatments to add additional interest or contrast to the finished arrangement. Be aware of the special nature of these materials before adding them to the design. For example, larger, heavier materials such as handmade paper will require stronger securing techniques; thin, light materials such as raffia are very easy to secure.

Making a Bow

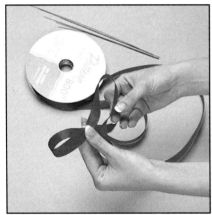 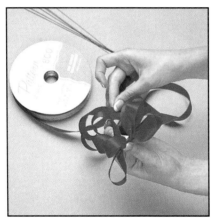 

1. Unroll several yards from a bolt of ribbon. Form loops from the ribbon with your right hand. Pinch the center of the loops with your left thumb and forefinger as you work.

2. Continue to add loops to your bow. Keep pinching the center of the bow with your left thumb and forefinger. After you have all the loops you desire (the more loops, the fuller the bow), trim away excess ribbon from the bolt. If you want a streamer, leave the ribbon longer before cutting.

3. Insert a length of wire through the center of the ribbon. Bring the two ends of the wire to the back so that it completely surrounds the bow. Twist the ends of the wire securely and tightly right next to the center of the bow to eliminate loop slippage. The wire can then be used to attach the bow to the wreath. You may also trim the wire and glue the bow in place.

Note: When using heavier ribbon, it is advisable to use a chenille stem to secure the bow in place. The tiny hairs on the chenille stem will hold the bow securely and not allow potential twisting of the bare wire. For tiny, delicate bows, thin cloth-covered wire can be used for securing. It eliminates slipping and is so tiny that it disappears into the bow loops.

Air Drying

Pick flowers that you plan to air dry at their peak of bloom or just before. Remove the leaves, since they become brittle and break off during the drying process. The flowers should be picked after the morning dew has dried, but before the hot sun has made the flowers droop.

To air dry flowers, combine six to 12 stems in a bundle with the heads at slightly different levels. Bind them all together with raffia, twine, or rubber bands. Hang the flowers upside down, tied to a beam, dowel, rod, or rafter. Allow plenty of space between bundles for proper air circulation. When selecting a location for hanging, choose a warm, dry, dark spot with good air circulation for moisture evaporation and color retention.

Check on your flowers often. Sometimes, the changes will be dramatic; other times, they will be barely noticeable. If you notice insect damage, mold, or mildew, remove the damaged flowers to eliminate spreading. As the flowers dry, the stems may shrink. You may need to tie them more tightly so that they do not slip away from their binding and fall to the floor.

Carefully watch the flowers to prevent overdrying. Some flowers will dry in three to five days; others will take up to three weeks. Test the flowers by touching to see if they are dry and rigid. Do not overdry! If they are dry, take them down and gently shake the bunch to get rid of excess dried materials and to eliminate shedding. When the flowers are completely dry, remove and place them in a cool, dry location away from direct heat and sunlight. After drying, flowers can be used individually in designs or simply tied with a lovely bow and displayed as is.

Glycerine

Preserving floral materials in a glycerine solution will keep the materials soft and supple for years. Normally, this technique is best when used with branches and leaves, but is also effective on small filler materials such as gypsophila (baby's breath).

Be sure to pick branches to be treated late in the season when they have full-sized leaves and mature, woody stems. When picked too early, they will droop and become unattractive. Don't put the stems in water after picking since any water drawn up will dilute the glycerine solution.

To make preserving solution, mix equal parts of glycerine and very hot water. Glycerine is fairly inexpensive and can be purchased at a local pharmacy. Mix the two parts thoroughly. If preserving branches, cut them between 15 and 24 inches long and split the stem so that it will draw in the solution faster.

Be sure the water is hot to assist with solution absorption. Place the branches in a heavy container with at least 6 inches of glycerine solution. Check the water level often and add additional water/glycerine solution as it evaporates.

When preserving sprays of leaves, use a large, flat container with 2 inches of glycerine solution. Place the leaves flat in the solution and weigh them down with sand or pebbles if they float to the top. Keep the solution at a constant level. Depending on the materials being preserved, it may take from ten days to six weeks for the solution to work its way through. You'll be able to watch the materials change color as the solution works its way to the top. When the entire stem has been preserved, remove it from the container and wipe dry.

Desiccants

Desiccants are moisture-absorbing substances. They include sand, borax, and silica gel. Sand has been used for centuries, and the finest grade is an excellent desiccant. Borax has larger granules that can cause damage to flowers. Although silica gel is the most expensive desiccant, it is also the fastest working and the finest in granular size, so it causes no damage to the materials. Desiccant-dried flowers usually retain their color very well.

For drying flowers with a desiccant, choose a plastic or glass container, since wood and cardboard may retain moisture. Cover the bottom of the container with about 1 inch of desiccant material. Bell- and cup-shaped flowers should be placed on their sides, while other flowers are best placed face-up in the desiccant mixture. Cut the stems short and allow generous spacing between flowers.

Gently cover the flowers with a layer of desiccant. Be careful not to bend the flower petals into unnatural shapes. Spooning the desiccant between multi-petaled flowers such as roses and carnations is an effective technique. You can place several layers of flowers in one container as long as each flower is completely surrounded by ample desiccant, and the drying times of the chosen varieties are similar. For extra protection, the container used should be completely secured from moisture in the air. Using either an airtight container or taping an existing container works well.

Delicate flowers take only three to four days, while larger flowers can take a week to ten days to dry. Remove the flowers by gently pouring off the desiccant and carefully lifting the flowers. With a small paint brush, remove any residue from the petals. If any petals have broken off, glue them on with white craft glue. You can also replace the stems with wires or tape the existing stems.

Some flowers, such as orchids and snapdragons, cannot be dried in any other way than with a desiccant. They should be layered in the desiccant and their deep throats completely filled with it.

Sometimes, it is best to mix different desiccants because of granule size and the amount of drying time. The best mixture is equal parts of silica gel crystals and sand. Since it is important that the desiccant be absolutely dry, silica gel offers the best assurance. Commercial silica gel contains blue crystals. As the gel absorbs moisture, the crystals turn a pale blue. Eventually, when they are at their limit of absorbing and need to be reactivated, they turn pink.

To reactivate silica gel, spread it on a cookie sheet and place it in a slightly warm oven. Shake the pan from time to time to distribute the crystals. When they turn blue again, they are ready to use. Keep the gel strained after use to remove any stray petals and store it in an airtight container. It will last for many years.

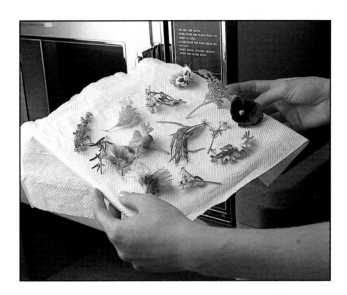

Microwave Drying

Remarkable results are achieved by drying flowers in the microwave together with the use of silica gel. Simply place a layer of silica gel in a nonmetal container. Put a paper towel over the top and cover it with floral materials. Sprinkle a generous amount of silica gel around and through the flowers. Do not wire any flowers before microwaving them.

Use a medium microwave setting. Small flowers will take one to two minutes, while larger ones may take three to four minutes. If they are not completely dry when removed, flowers can be placed back in the microwave for additional time. Allow the flowers standing time when you remove them. Stems can be wired, floral-taped, or glued on after drying. Store the flowers with a small amount of silica gel to avoid moisture absorption.

Creating Dried Flower Arrangements

Remember that dried flowers will not look the same as they did in their fresh state. Many flowers change colors when dried, either becoming a neutral color or a deeper color tone than the original flower. The actual flowers and leaves will also often change shape. Some normally straight leaves will curl; others will remain the same. Certain flower petals will turn inward, even though they were straight and upright in their original state.

One of the most striking differences is in the sizes of the materials after they have been dried. Baby's breath, for example, shrinks approximately 75 percent after drying. Most other flowers, stems, and leaves also shrink as their moisture evaporates.

The strength of floral materials also changes after drying. Many petaled flowers, such as daisies, become extremely fragile and fall apart easily. They should be used sparingly and delicately.

As you continue drying and preserving flowers, keep lists of the techniques and drying times that work best for the materials you commonly use. You'll find that you will use flowers most common in your area or even in your own garden. Experiment, have fun, enjoy!

Country Basket

An abundance of airy dried and preserved materials fill this country-style wicker basket. The bunny tails are added in groups instead of single stems to create more of an impact. Soft, pleasing color tones blend together beautifully to enhance the whitewashed look of this basket. Natural and fresh-looking materials are always the best choices for country-style design.

1. Glue the dry foam in the basket and cover it with Spanish moss. Fill the basket with the starburst gypsophila, creating a large circular mass.

2. Randomly fill the basket with the pink roses, pink carnation heads, nigella, and pink pennyroyal. Add the purple bunny tails grouped in fours with wood picks (see page 7). Make a large bow (see page 8) from the 4 yards of pink moire ribbon. Attach it to the base of the handle with florist wire.

Materials

12-inch long oval whitewashed basket
1 block of dry foam
hot glue gun
glue sticks
handful of Spanish moss
1½ bunches of preserved starburst gypsophila (or glycerine-treated baby's breath)

12 dried pink long-stem roses
12 dried large pink carnation heads
½ bunch of dried nigella
¼ bunch of dried pink pennyroyal
36 dried purple bunny tails
wood picks
4 yards of 1-inch wide pink moire ribbon
florist wire

1. Starting at the handle, glue a band of gypsophila and plumosus around the perimeter of the basket with the hot glue gun.

2. Add the purple statice and white and pink rosebuds evenly. Glue them into place with a slight dab of hot glue on the stems, gently burying them into the gypsophila. Repeat the same step with some of the pink carnation heads and pink spray roses.

3. Glue a larger spray of gypsophila along the base of the handle. Fill in the area with the remaining gypsophila, roses, and carnation heads. Repeat on the other side.

4. Fill the basket with potpourri (or line it with foil and fill it with green plants). Take the 2 colors of ribbon and wrap them around the handle. Make bows on each side of the handle base (see page 8) and secure them with hot glue.

Materials	
8-inch long oval natural woven basket	6 dried large white and pink rosebuds
hot glue gun	9 dried mini pink carnation heads
glue sticks	4 stems of dried pink spray roses
3 stems of preserved super fine gypsophila (baby's breath)	potpourri of choice
1 stem of preserved plumosus	3 yards of ¼-inch pink satin ribbon
2 stems of dried purple statice	3 yards of ³/₁₆-inch white picot ribbon

Potpourri Basket

Delicate dried and preserved flowers circle the edges of a wicker basket, and tiny bouquets gently adorn each handle. Sweet-smelling potpourri makes this basket extra special by bringing a lovely aroma to the area in which it is displayed. Use a variety of dried flower petals to change the colors and scents of the potpourri. In time, its smell will dissipate. Simply add a few drops of potpourri oil to the mixture to rejuvenate the aroma.

A richly textured basket is the ideal choice for this exquisite selection of dried flowers. This arrangement makes a bold statement with flower clusters and tall, narrow flowers in the center. The delicate carnations and roses nestled at opposite sides of the design add a charming sense of balance.

1. Attach the block of dry foam in the basket with the hot glue. Moss lightly, securing it with the greening pins. Place the 3 purple delphiniums vertically in the back third of the basket. Add the mauve canella to the lower left of the handle, allowing it to cascade down over the side of the basket.

2. To the right of the delphiniums, place the 12 pink roses in a tight triangular grouping working from top to bottom. Add the 3 deep rose peonies at the lower right-hand side of the basket handle.

3. Place the lavender in the center along the handle. Secure several stems at a time with wood picks (see page 7). Add purple statice to separate the lavender from the peonies. Fill in any voids with red happy flowers.

4. To the left of the delphiniums, place the 10 pink snapdragons in a triangular fashion. Fill the void between the canella and the snapdragons with the white carnations.

5. Fill in any remaining voids with heather on the right-hand side of the roses and burgundy strawflowers toward the back of the arrangement.

Materials:
10-inch long natural woven basket
1 block of dry foam
hot glue gun
glue sticks
handful of Spanish moss
greening pins
3 dried large purple delphiniums
½ bunch of dried mauve canella
12 dried pink roses
3 dried deep rose peonies
1 bunch of dried lavender
wood picks
1 spray of dried purple statice
½ bunch of dried red happy flowers or star flowers
10 dried pink snapdragons
8 dried white carnations
⅓ bunch of dried heather
3 stems of dried burgundy strawflowers

Elegant Chinese Basket

Mirrored Wreath

You can enhance any home decor with a flower-embellished mirror.
Use rounded flowers of your choice to create a uniform design.
Tiny ribbons entwined throughout encourage eye movement as they
visually carry the viewer around the wreath. Add a full bow to
the arrangement if you wish. This design can be equally beautiful
without the mirror.

1. Cover the wreath base very lightly with Spanish moss, securing it with greening pins.

2. Evenly distribute the preserved plumosus, springerii, gypsophila, purple statice, and eucalyptus.

3. Add the roses (red, pink, and pink spray), white carnations, and thistle, keeping an even distribution of color and texture.

4. Glue the mirror to the back of the wreath base with a hot glue gun. Softly weave the cream and burgundy ribbons around the wreath by loosely drooping them. Secure the ribbons with greening pins.

Materials

12-inch dry foam wreath base	12 dried pink roses
handful of Spanish moss	3 stems of dried pink spray roses
greening pins	12 dried white carnations
3 stems of preserved plumosus	1 stem of preserved thistle
3 stems of preserved springerii	10-inch round mirror
3 stems of dried gypsophila (baby's breath)	hot glue gun
	glue sticks
1 stem of dried purple statice	3½ yards of each: ¼-inch wide
1 stem of preserved eucalyptus	cream and burgundy ribbon
6 dried red roses	

Romantic Wreath

A heart-shaped vine wreath can be the perfect expression of your
love whenever you feel romantic. As an attractive vertical design
accents one side of the wreath, loops and loops of tiny ribbon act
as filler and add color to the wreath. This pretty picture is completed
with cream-colored flowers and delicate pink and purple dried materials.

1. Glue the dry foam into the pouch of the wreath with the hot glue gun. Cover it with moss and secure with greening pins.

2. On the left-hand side of the pouch, add 3 stems of artemisia and 3 stems of pink pennyroyal.

3. Add the 6 large red rosebuds to the left-hand side of the pouch, working with the more tightly closed buds at the top and the more open ones at the bottom. Cluster the purple statice in the center of the pouch. On the right-hand side of the wreath, gently curve the pink spray roses, following the natural curve of the heart.

4. Make a bow from 1 yard of the pink and ivory ribbons (see page 8). Attach it to the top of the heart with the hot glue gun. Wrap streamers from the ribbon along the right-hand side of the heart. Add another bow made from 1 yard of the pink and ivory ribbons. Attach it to the right-hand side of the heart. Continue with streamers along the lower right-hand side of the wreath. Make a bow from 1½ yards of the pink and ivory ribbons and attach it to the bottom of the heart with the hot glue gun.

Materials

12-inch heart-shaped wreath with pouch	3 stems of dried artemisia
2 × 1-inch piece of dry foam	3 stems of dried pink pennyroyal
hot glue gun	6 dried large red rosebuds
glue sticks	1 stem of dried purple statice
handful of Spanish moss	4 stems of dried pink spray roses
greening pins	3½ yards of each: ¼-inch pink and ivory ribbon

Yuletide Wreath

Rings of untwisted paper ribbon form the base of this Christmas wreath made of natural materials. The deep reds and greens create a feeling of traditional elegance. The preserved greenery and eucalyptus add the necessary color and texture. Another season could easily be celebrated with this same basic idea. Just use spring flowers, a lighter-colored wreath, and a lively looking bird.

1. Glue the dry foam to the bottom right of the wreath using the hot glue gun. Fasten it with wire. Cover the foam lightly with Spanish moss and secure it with greening pins.

2. Insert the red cedar roses vertically, one below the next. Also add the preserved eucalyptus vertically.

3. Layer 3 mushrooms in a terracing fashion from bottom to top, starting from largest to smallest. Insert the remaining mushroom at a 45-degree angle at the right of the block of foam.

4. Insert the juniper and cedar in an S-shaped curve from top left to bottom right. Use wood picks if necessary (see page 7).

5. Wood pick and tape clusters of the red star flowers and red edelweiss. Insert them in the arrangement, following the curves and lines of the greenery.

Materials:
18-inch red rope and vine wreath (or any other 18-inch wreath)
3 × 3-inch block of dry foam
hot glue gun
glue sticks
floral wire
handful of Spanish moss
greening pins
6 dried red cedar roses (or other dried pod flowers sprayed red)
6 stems of preserved eucalyptus
4 dried sponge mushrooms
2 stems of preserved juniper
4 stems of preserved cedar
wood picks
florist tape
½ bunch of dried red star flowers
½ bunch of dried red edelweiss (or red button flowers)

Straw Hat Chic

Hats are HOT! Hang one on your wall, place one near a sitting area, or create a hat stand just to showcase your favorite. The versatility of hat designs is amazing. You can either add flowers in a crescent design as shown or completely surround the crown for a more abundant look. Use dried materials in the colors highlighted in wallpapers, rugs, draperies, and other room accents to create a coordinating decoration.

1. Attach the 1½-yard length of ribbon around the band of the hat using a hot glue gun.

2. Glue on the gypsophila with the hot glue gun. Begin at the knot of the ribbon and work your way about two-thirds of the way around the band. Add a little bit of plumosus to the gypsophila.

3. Attach the pink spray roses, white carnation heads, and pink rose heads with the hot glue gun. Again start at the knot, but as you work your way out, apply the flowers less heavily to form a crescent around the band. Fill in with the blue pennygrass.

4. Using the 2½-yard length of ribbon, make a soft bow (see page 8) and attach it with the hot glue gun.

Materials:

straw hat, approximately 14 inches across

4 yards of 1-inch wide lace over blue satin ribbon divided into one 1½-yard piece and one 2½-yard piece

hot glue gun

glue sticks

4 stems of glycerine-treated or dried gypsophila (baby's breath)

1 stem of glycerine-treated plumosus

3 stems of dried pink spray roses (about 24 buds in various stages of bloom)

9 dried mini white carnation heads

5 dried large pink rose heads

1 stem of dried blue pennygrass

25

Bridal Bouquet Keepsake

An heirloom doily tucked into the base of a bouquet tastefully accents its delicate nature, just as the long stems of the flowers and greenery help create a clustering effect. To complete the elegant look of this design, the stems of the white bridal roses are bound with white satin ribbon. What better way to remember a wedding day?

1. Arrange the white roses and scabiosas in a bouquet. Form a collar around the flowers with the plumosus.

2. Hand-tie the bouquet with 1 yard of the ½-inch wide satin picot ribbon.

3. Wrap the 1-inch wide ribbon around the stems. Tie on the doilies with the remaining yard of the ½-inch wide ribbon. Finish binding the stems, covering the doily ties.

4. To dry, remove the 1-inch wide ribbon covering the stems and hang the bouquet upside down in a warm, dry, and dark place.

Materials

25 fresh white bridal roses
1 bunch of fresh scabiosas
4 to 5 stems of fresh plumosus
2 yards of ½-inch wide ivory satin picot ribbon

1 yard of 1-inch wide ivory satin ribbon
two 10-inch ivory lace doilies

European Hand-Tied Bouquet

The trick to creating a perfect hand-tied bouquet is to place the stems in a spiraling fashion so they hook into each other and continually widen the base of the bouquet. Remember to use long, narrow materials in the center and shorter, fuller materials to create the outside diameter. Be careful when cutting the stems of the flowers—properly cut stems allow the bouquet to stand on its own.

1. Hold the bunch of chicory vertically. Gradually add 5 dark red peonies, gently turning the arrangement at about a 70-degree angle. Add the 12 pink carnations; turn the arrangement again. Do the same with 5 stems of pink larkspur, the remaining 5 peonies, and the other 5 stems of larkspur. When finished, you should have gone full circle with the flowers, creating a tepee effect. Secure the stems with florist wire.

2. Starting at a lower level, add ½ bunch of pink spray roses and turn the bouquet approximately 70 degrees. Add the bunch of lavender in the center, remembering that it will be the focal point of the bouquet. Turn the bouquet. Add 2 hydrangeas, turning the bouquet again. Add the second half of the spray roses, turn, and add the last 2 hydrangeas. Turn again. Once again, you will have gone full circle with the flowers, creating a tepee effect. Gently add the plumosus, forming a collar around the dried flowers. Secure the arrangement with florist wire.

3. Tie the bouquet tightly several times with the raffia. Make a soft bow from the burlap (see page 8), and attach it to the raffia bow with wire. Trim the stems evenly with pruners or scissors, and spread them so that the arrangement stands by itself.

Materials:
1 bunch of dried chicory
10 dried dark red peonies
12 dried pink carnations
10 stems of dried pink larkspur
florist wire
1 bunch of dried pink spray roses, divided into half
1 bunch of dried lavender
4 dried hydrangeas
7 stems of preserved plumosus
twelve 1-yard strands of raffia
3 yards of soft blue burlap ribbon
pruners or scissors

Miniature Flower Tree

Materials:
3-inch clay pot
handful of rocks
1 block of dry foam
hot glue gun
glue sticks
18- to 22-inch pieces of dry branches (or a ½-inch dowel rod cut to size)
handful of sheet moss
handful of Spanish moss
greening pins
4 stems of dried plumosus
2 stems of dried or preserved gypsophila (baby's breath)
12 dried pink roses
12 dried mini red carnations
2 stems of dried pink larkspur
2 stems of dried pink spray roses
2 yards of each: ¼-inch satin cream and burgundy ribbon
florist wire

A foam ball glued to a stick is the simple base for creating dried arrangements in a circular form. Use natural twigs and ribbon streamers to create eye movement and to help connect the container with the floral arrangement visually. This striking design is perfect for home and party decorating! For a different twist, select colors that enhance those in a room. Add additional accents to coordinate with the type of party planned—butterflies for spring, rattles for baby showers, and doves for weddings.

1. Fill the 3-inch pot about half-full with rocks. Carve a piece of dry foam to fit into the 3-inch pot. Glue it into the pot and let it dry. Sink the dry branches into the foam, gluing them in. Cover the top of the foam with sheet moss.

2. Carve a 3½-inch ball from the dry foam and push it in about 2 inches into the top of the branch. Glue it in for security. Moss the ball lightly with Spanish moss, securing it with greening pins.

3. Cover the ball with 1- to 3-inch lengths of dried plumosus, saving a few lengths. Be careful to add them evenly.

5. Attach a small cluster of dried flowers and greenery that you saved to the bottom of the branches. Make a bow (see page 8) from 1½ yards of cream and burgundy ribbon, attaching it to the base of the ball with florist wire. Add another bow, made of the remaining ½-yard of cream and burgundy ribbon, attaching it to the top of the clay pot with florist wire.

4. Insert the gypsophila, pink roses, red carnations, pink larkspur, and pink spray roses evenly on the ball; save a few stems.

What could be more elegant than a rosebud-studded topiary designed for Christmas? One that has an assortment of greens to add variety in texture and form and long streamers of ribbon to carry the eye down the tree effectively! For a different look, vary the selection of colors. Rich Victorian colors, such as peach, mauve, and French blue, can create a striking design.

1. Spray the clay pot red and the styrofoam cone green with the quick-drying floral paint (or hobby or spray paint). Allow to dry. Shape the ⅓-block of foam to fit into the clay pot. Glue it in using the hot glue gun. Insert the twig into the base of the styrofoam cone, making sure it is centered. Secure with hot glue. Insert the other end of the twig into the dry foam, leaving about a 3- to 4-inch tree trunk. Secure with hot glue. Cover the dry foam with Spanish moss.

2. Evenly distribute 2- to 3-inch pieces of springerii, plumosus, boxwood, cedar, and ming fern over the styrofoam cone. Make sure to use smaller pieces at the top and longer, fuller pieces at the bottom.

3. Using smaller pieces at the top and longer, fuller pieces at the bottom, evenly distribute the red roses over the entire tree. Repeat with some of the red pepper berries and clusters of red star flowers. Attach wood picks (see page 7), if necessary.

4. Make a bow from 2 yards of the red ribbon (see page 8). Drape it over the top of the topiary to look like a garland. Make another bow from the remaining 1 yard of red ribbon and the 1 yard of green ribbon. Attach to the base with florist wire. Insert a cluster of pepper berries next to the ribbon.

Materials

3- to 4-inch diameter clay pot	2 stems of dried boxwood
12-inch styrofoam cone	1 twig of preserved cedar
quick-drying red floral spray paint	2 to 3 stems of preserved ming fern
quick-drying green floral spray paint	2 dozen dried red roses
⅓-block of dry foam	2 to 3 stems of dried red pepper berries
hot glue gun	1 bunch of dried red star flowers
glue sticks	wood picks
6- to 7-inch twig	3 yards of ¼-inch wide red ribbon
handful of Spanish moss	1 yard of ⅜-inch wide green ribbon
3 stems of preserved springerii	florist wire
4 stems of preserved plumosus	

Holiday Cheer Topiary

Autumn Harvest Planter

Deep green, rustic brown, and goldenrod yellow accent the natural colorations found in the terra cotta container. The wheat and cattails gracefully establish the height and shape of the overall design. A fluffy open weave bow enhances the focal area. You can vary the same style of design with a multitude of materials suited to any holiday by simply changing the container used.

1. Glue dry foam into the turkey planter with the hot glue gun. Cover it with Spanish moss. Add the 8 cattails in one bunch to create vertical height. Place the pennygrass as if to outline the tail of the turkey.

2. Add yarrow, wheat, barley, protea flats, thistle, and celosia as desired to fill in the empty spaces. Secure stems with wood picks as needed (see page 7). Make a bow from the burlap ribbon (see page 8) and attach it to the left of the turkey's head.

Materials

8-inch terra cotta turkey planter	½ bunch of dried wheat
½-block of dry foam	½ bunch of dried barley
hot glue gun	2 dried curly protea flats
glue sticks	3 pieces of dried thistle
handful of Spanish moss	3 pieces of dried celosia
8 cattails	wood picks
½ bunch of dried blue pennygrass	1 yard of 1-inch wide light blue burlap ribbon
½ bunch of dried mini yarrow	

Jack-O'-Lantern

A smiling Jack-O'-Lantern container is ideally suited for this striking design with well-established horizontal and vertical lines. Raffia ribbons complete the balance. A bright candle inside this happy face will surely delight the hearts of young and old during the Halloween season. Spread leaves and additional raffia ribbon around the base to create greater visual impact.

1. Glue the dry foam to the inverted hat of the Jack-O'-Lantern. Set the inverted hat on top of the pumpkin head and moss lightly. Secure the moss with greening pins. Cut the rust-colored wheat in half and insert each half horizontally into the sides of the foam.

2. Place the dock vertically in the center of the arrangement. Add the strawflowers from the base of the hat and work upwards. Place the bronze canella in the lower right-hand corner, allowing it to cascade downward. Fill in with brown oak leaves, love grass, and protea green as desired.

3. Make a bow from the raffia (see page 8) and attach it to the right-hand side of the Jack-O'-Lantern with wire.

Materials

7-inch terra cotta Jack-O'-Lantern	3 stems of dried strawflowers
3 × 5-inch piece of dry foam	1 twig of dried bronze canella
hot glue gun	2 stems of preserved brown oak leaves
glue sticks	
handful of Spanish moss	1 stem of dried love grass
greening pins	1 stem of dricd protea green
9 pieces of dried rust-colored wheat	4 strings of peach raffia ribbon
3 stems of dried dock	florist wire

This delightful gift can be easily created for a friend or loved one on that special day. Gift bags in a variety of patterns and sizes are easily purchased at specialty or gift shops. They make memorable containers for dried and preserved flower arrangements. To give someone a truly personal gift, why not arrange flowers that you picked yourself?

1. Glue the ¾-block of dry foam in the decorative paper gift tote with the hot glue gun and cover it with Spanish moss.

2. Fill the entire bag with candytuft, making sure to work in a triangular pattern. Add the 4 stems of plumosus.

3. Place 1 sprig of lemon grass in the center of the arrangement. Add a grouping of 3 mauve artemisias in the back center to establish height. Wood pick the stems, if necessary (see page 7). Add the mauve liatris to the left of the center for added texture. Put the 3 mauve peonies in the lower left-hand side to establish the focal point.

4. Fill the line from the top of the lemon grass to the peonies with a cluster of the mini red carnations. On the other side of the arrangement, add the large pink carnations, purple larkspur, purple statice, and heather, making sure to work in a triangular pattern. Make a bow from the two shades of ribbon (see page 8). Attach it to the lower right-hand corner with florist wire.

Materials

8 × 10-inch decorative paper gift tote	wood picks
¾-block of dry foam	1 dried mauve liatris
hot glue gun	3 dried mauve peonies
glue sticks	6 dried mini red carnations
handful of Spanish moss	7 dried large pink carnations
1⅓ bunches of glycerine-treated candytuft (or glycerine-treated baby's breath)	4 stems of dried purple larkspur
	2 stems of dried purple statice
	2 stems of dried heather
4 stems of preserved plumosus (or springerii)	1½ yards of each: 1-inch wide burgundy picot and mauve picot ribbon
1 sprig of dried lemon grass	florist wire
3 stems of dried mauve artemisia	

Flowers in the Bag

Trendy Handmade Paper Design

Using handmade paper with flowers you have dried yourself is a wonderful way to create an exciting design. Notice the way some of the dried materials coordinate with the larger paper runner, while others are accented by the lighter color of the smaller runner. You can create a natural-looking Christmas design by using red, green, gold, and silver. Any special accents are completely up to you!

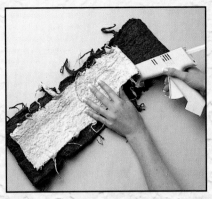

1. Glue the narrower strip of paper ribbon on top of the wider strip using the glue gun. Make sure that the dark border is even.

2. Place a heavy spray of hot glue in the center of the paper ribbon. Quickly place the 4 long sprigs of eucalyptus in an X-formation on the hot glue.

3. Glue the 3 sprays of flowering eucalyptus, filling in the spaces between the preserved eucalyptus. Add the 3 dark pink carnation heads in a triangular placement. Also add the 4 red rose heads.

Materials

19 × 4-inch piece of cream paper ribbon

23 × 6-inch piece of dark purple paper ribbon

hot glue gun

glue sticks

5 sprigs of preserved eucalyptus; four 8-inch lengths and one 4-inch length

3 sprays of dried flowering eucalyptus

3 dried dark pink carnation heads

4 dried red rose heads

4 stems of 4- to 6-inch long dried red spray roses

4 dried mini light pink carnations

2 sprigs of dried heather

3 yards of 1-inch wide burgundy ribbon

4. Fill in the voids with red spray roses, remaining eucalyptus, mini pink carnations, and heather. Add a soft bow in the center (see page 8). Glue it in with the hot glue gun.

Christmas Centerpiece

Horizontal floral sprays are commonly used to accent the space above a window or door. When they are as large as this one, they create a striking design to adorn a mantel or fireplace. The white branches can be cut from your own backyard trees and painted white. A large, full bow adds a festive touch for holiday cheer!

Materials:
8 white sprayed birch branches
binding twine
4 stems of preserved eucalyptus
2 stems of preserved balsam
3 stems of preserved ming fern
hot glue gun
glue sticks
3 dried curly protea flats
2 sprays of dried mini white carnations
5 dried large red carnations
2 stems of dried red pepper berries
2 yards of 1-inch wide red velvet ribbon
2 artificial red cardinals (optional)

1. Tie the sprayed birch branches together in a criss-cross manner and secure them with binding twine.

2. Add the eucalyptus, balsam, and ming fern, following the shape of the branches. Secure them with a hot glue gun.

3. Add the protea flats in a triangular pattern, securing them with hot glue. Place the mini white carnations and some red carnations so they radiate from the center. Add some of the red pepper berries.

4. Bind the entire arrangement with the red velvet ribbon. Add a soft bow to the center (see page 8). Adorn the bow with the remaining pepper berries and carnations. Glue the two birds on opposite ends of the arrangement, if desired.

Traditional Japanese Ikebana

The striking beauty of the container draws special attention to itself in this arrangement. If dried equisetum is unavailable, fresh can be used since it dries beautifully after being attached to the container. The delicate forsythia, curly willow, and strelitzia leaves are a perfect choice for this elegant design.

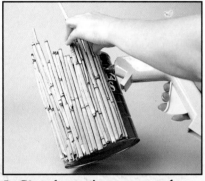

1. Glue the equisetum onto the coffee can, leaving some pieces longer to hang over the top edge of the can.

2. Glue the dry foam to the inside of the can. Cover the top with sheet moss and attach it with greening pins.

3. Add the curly willow in its natural curve on the sides of container. Place the large strelitzia leaves in the center. Frame them with 3 mini strelitzia leaves in a triangular pattern. Add the forsythias to the left. Place 2 mini strelitzia leaves in the lower right-hand side, letting them fall from the front of the container.

Materials

39-ounce coffee can	handful of sheet moss
2 bunches equisetum, cut into pieces the height of the can	greening pins
hot glue gun	3 branches of dried curly willow
glue sticks	2 dried large strelitzia leaves
1 block of dry foam	5 dried mini strelitzia leaves
	5 stems of dried forsythia

Southwest Design

These exotic materials are not commonly found in our gardens, yet they are beautiful when used for dried floral designs. They are readily available in floral and craft shops. To draw our eye to the center of the design, two cut palmetto leaves are inserted vertically.

1. Glue the foam into the container using the hot glue gun. Moss lightly, securing it with greening pins.

2. Add the green bear grass to the back center of the foam. Wood pick and tape the cane coils (see page 7). Add the 3 peach cane coils to the left of the bear grass to establish the vertical line. These should be equidistant from each other, the bottom coil about 6 inches from the base and the top coil about 18 inches high.

3. Establish the focal point with the peach lotus pods, placing one in the center of the arrangement and the other flowing from the left of the container. Place one green palmetto leaf behind the first lotus pod. Add the second leaf so that the top of the first is at the bottom of the second.

4. Add the peach yucca canes to the back left of the arrangement, allowing the bottom one to fall naturally. Place the peach milo sea branches to the right of the bottom lotus blossom. Add the peach strelitzia leaves to the right of the lotus pod and the peach cane spring behind the milo sea leaves.

Materials

4½ × 10½-inch ceramic forest-green container	wood picks
⅓-block of dry foam	florist tape
hot glue gun	2 dried peach lotus pods
glue sticks	2 dried cut green palmetto leaves
handful of Spanish moss	2 pieces of dried peach yucca cane
greening pins	1 large stem of dried peach milo sea branches, broken into 3 pieces
24 stems of dried green bear grass	2 dried peach strelitzia leaves
3 dried peach cane coils	1 dried peach cane spring

Country Pots

Natural and free-flowing is the way to describe this marvelous design.
The unplanned look of the finished piece gives us a casual feeling
and makes it appropriate in both semi-formal and informal settings.
The design can be enhanced seasonally with the addition of spring
birds, summer seashells, fall pumpkins, and pine branches in winter.

Materials

six to eight ½- to 1-inch diameter branches

hot glue gun

glue sticks

handful of sheet moss

handful of Spanish moss

one 4½-inch clay pot

four 3½-inch clay pots

two 1½-inch clay pots

floral clay

1 block of dry foam

12 dried mini white carnations

1 stem of dried purple statice

4 stems of dried lavender

5 sprays of dried mini red carnations

1 stem of dried leptospermum

1 sprig of dried heather

1 sprig of dried lepidium

3 to 4 stems of preserved springerii

18 dried white roses

2 stems of dried leatherleaf

2 stems of dried tree fern

1 stem of dried pink spray roses

2 dried birch twigs

14 dried clovers

1. Arrange the branches in an unusual configuration. Secure with hot glue. Cover with sheet moss and Spanish moss, as desired.

2. Place the clay pots in a random arrangement. Place some upright, others sideways. Secure with hot glue and floral clay.

3. Glue a piece of dry foam in each little pot. Cover the foam with Spanish moss. Fill the pots with the appropriate dried flowers, as follows:

 4½-inch pot—12 mini white carnations, 1 stem of purple statice, 3 stems of lavender
 3½-inch pot—5 sprays of mini red carnations, 1 stem of leptospermum, 1 sprig of heather, 1 sprig of lepidium
 3½-inch pot—3 to 4 stems of preserved springerii
 3½-inch pot—12 white roses, 1 stem of lavender
 3½-inch pot—6 white roses, 2 stems of leatherleaf, 2 stems of tree fern
 1½-inch pot—1 stem of pink spray roses, 1 birch twig
 1½-inch pot—14 clovers, 1 birch twig

4. Weave the birch twigs in and out of the pots by bending them. Secure them with hot glue.

Pavé for the 1990s

An upscale approach to dried flower arranging is showcased by the use of the pavé technique. Pavé means that the flower stems are cut short and inserted in a compact fashion. The process resembles the paving of a brick road when the bricks are placed side by side. Vertical placements of strelitzia leaves, rosebuds, and lotus pods draw our eye into the focal area.

1. Glue the block of foam into the container. Cover the top with the three mosses, giving the effect of a wooded area. Use greening pins to secure the mosses.

2. Insert one 20-inch white strelitzia leaf about two-thirds of the way back on the foam block. Cut the second strelitzia leaf to 12 inches and place it about 1 inch in front and to the left of the first. Add one white lotus pod low in the center of the container. Leave the other lotus pod about 10 inches high and place it just behind the first one. Terrace the burgundy sea grape leaves in the lower right-hand side, resting the lowest one on the rim of the container.

3. Place 7 red roses in a vertical line starting at the top of the lower lotus pod and working 18 inches upward. Fill the lower left-hand side with the remaining roses. Use the pavé technique, which means placing the roses very tightly and evenly at the base of the arrangement.

4. Closely layer the pink celosia between the sea grape leaves and the lower lotus pod. Add the evergreen along the stem of the taller lotus pod. Pavé the right-hand side with the red carnations.

Materials

7 × 4-inch black ceramic container	2 dried white strelitzia leaves (at least 20 inches long)
½-block of dry foam	2 dried white lotus pods (with stems)
hot glue gun	
glue sticks	3 dried burgundy sea grape leaves
handful each of Spanish moss, reindeer moss, and sheet moss	18 dried red roses
greening pins	2 pieces of dried pink celosia
	1 stem of preserved evergreen
	3 dried red carnations

Pressed Flowers

Pressing Techniques

The art of pressing flowers is over 300 years old. It seems that the method was first invented by a botanist who wanted to preserve his plant specimens during study. Pressing flowers is an alternative method for drying and preserving. However, the resulting flowers can only be used to create flat, two-dimensional designs.

Pressing floral materials is easy, yet offers two unique challenges. First, you must locate materials that will work well arranged on a flat surface. Flowers that are not too deep or bulky in the center and do not retain a good deal of water in their petals (such as orchids) work best. Grow your own flowers and plants, visit your local florist or nursery, or even take long walks through wooded and wild areas to find flowers.

Equipment needed for pressing flowers is minimal. Blotting paper or highly absorbent paper is a must. Paper towels and tissue paper will work for small, thin items. Do not choose paper with a weave—it will transfer to the item you are pressing. For large items such as leaves, use newspaper; place them under chair cushions or mattresses to press.

Originally, flowers were placed between the pages of large books. This can still be done. However, you must check to be sure that the ink of the book will not transfer to the floral materials. Moisture from the floral material should also not transfer to the pages of the book. It is best to place a few sheets of absorbent paper between the pages and the floral materials.

A flower press is the best method for pressing flowers. Commercial flower presses are usually held in place with screws on each corner of the press. When using this type of press, be careful that equal pressure is applied to all four sides so that the materials press uniformly.

When choosing flowers to press, be adventurous. The process is inexpensive, so you can afford to try new and different ideas. Flower and leaf materials that are thin to start with give the best results. Those with moist, fleshy leaves and flowers are usually a disappointment, since the blotting paper cannot come in contact with the entire material and the flower will press poorly. Buttercups, clematis, pansy, Queen Anne's lace, and ivy are but a few varieties that work extremely well.

The calices of daisies and similar flowers may need to be slit before placing them in the press. Press carnation and rose petals individually. They can then be used singly or reassembled for display. Cut larger flowers such as daffodils in half for drying. Keep in mind that the pressed materials need not resemble an actual flower to be beautiful and appreciated.

Retaining the original coloring in flowers can be difficult. One way to help this process is to change the blotting papers two to three times in the first week. The wet papers can be dried and reused. A pair of tweezers, preferably plastic, will help in the movement of the flowers before and after pressing. A small camel's hair paint brush is great for moving delicate materials. It also helps prevent bruising that can cause an ugly brown stain.

Blue flowers traditionally have the most difficult color to retain. However, a few, such as delphinium florets, lobelia, pansies, and *Geranium ibericum,* do very well. Flowers in the red family deepen in color or fade considerably. Sometimes, the flowers used will turn a deep purple and, other times, the colors will change to a deep rose-pink shade. Yellow flowers usually work very well and retain their beautiful sunshine-bright color. Some that you may wish to try include buttercups, marigold petals, primroses, chrysanthemum petals, and daffodils. White flowers will turn varying shades of cream or ivory. If you wish to enhance the colors of your pressed materials, you can use watercolors and a soft brush.

Usually, leaves and other greenery deepen in color tones and even take on a hint of brown. Keep in mind, however, that the materials chosen should be selected as much for their overall shape as for their color. Since most of the floral materials take on a new shade of color, they will be uniform in look and will blend together well. Design your creations with the new neutral color tones in mind, using shape and texture as design components.

Pressed flowers will last a long time if cared for properly. Before arranging, place pressed materials between layers of fresh tissue and keep them in boxes located in a warm, dry area. If they reabsorb moisture, they may discolor and mold. Add a spoonful of silica gel crystals in a cloth sack to the box to help reabsorb any moisture.

You can easily make your own press with the use of two thin pieces of plywood, layers of thick cardboard, blotting paper, and two belts or harnesses. You can create any size flower press you wish as long as your wood, paper, and cardboard are of uniform size.

1. Place a piece of cardboard on top of the wood and a sheet of blotting paper on the cardboard. Arrange your floral materials on top of the blotting paper.

2. Put a second sheet of paper on top of the floral materials, then a piece of cardboard. Begin again with additional layers of materials in the same order.

3. After all the layers are arranged, place the second piece of plywood on top of everything, securing the belts snugly around the unit. Adequate pressure should be used to flatten materials, but be careful not to crush the materials being pressed.

Put the flower press in a warm, dry environment for at least six months. The longer the materials are allowed to dry in this location, the less likely their color is to fade when used in a design.

Dusty rose and French blue moire ribbon strips are a great beginning for a floral bookmark. Make sure to use a variety of textures to add interest and contrast. This idea can be taken one step further and expanded to be a table runner for a special gathering. Adorn the runner with bouquets of dried materials.

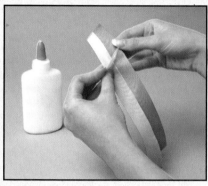

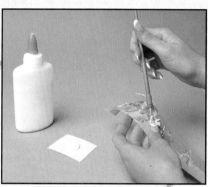

1. Glue the two ¾-inch strips of mauve and blue ribbon over the 1½-inch wide white ribbon using the white craft glue. Make sure to avoid air bubbles.

2. Using tweezers, arrange the pressed flowers (see pages 52-53) as desired in a long vertical pattern. Glue them on using the white craft glue and soft art brush. Remove the excess with a toothpick. Let dry.

3. Place the bookmark face forward on the sticky side of the clear Contac® paper, after you have removed the backing. Fold over, making sure that both the front and back have no air bubbles. Trim the Contac® paper with scissors to the size of the bookmark.

Materials

9-inch lengths of ¾-inch wide moire ribbon in mauve and blue

9-inch length of 1½-inch wide white ribbon

1 stem of pressed Queen Anne's lace

1 stem of pressed fern

1 pressed larkspur bud

white craft glue

tweezers

soft art brush

toothpicks

12 × 6-inch piece of clear Contac® paper

Victorian Floral Bookmark

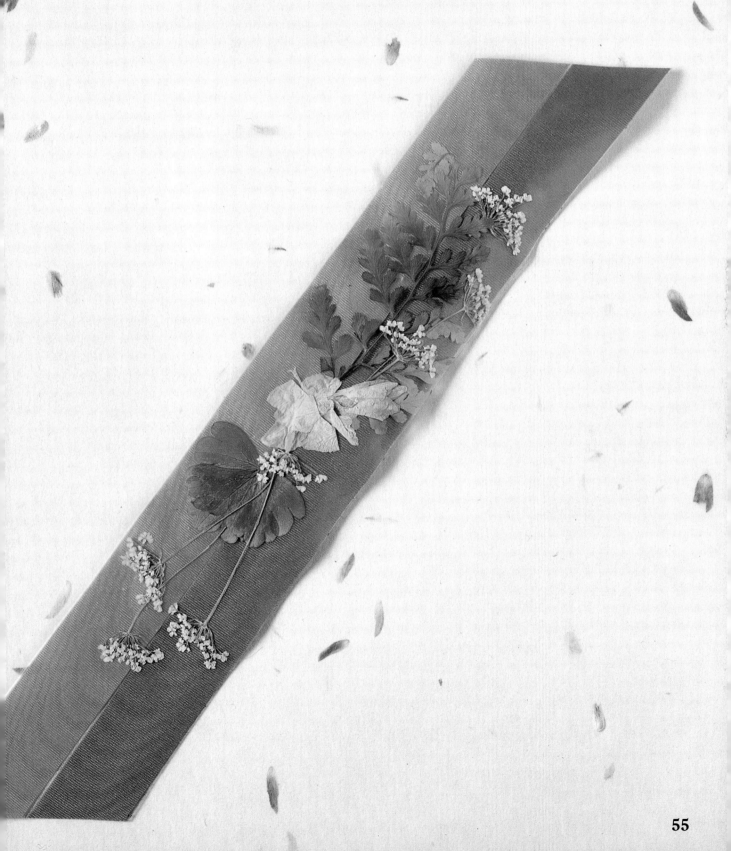

Elegant Greeting Card

Cream-colored paper is the background for an artistic floral arrangement created with pressed flowers. For an even more personal appeal, scent the stationery by enclosing it with a sachet of potpourri in a tightly sealed container for a minimum of four weeks. Add a tiny floral bud to the front of the envelope for interest.

1. Using tweezers, place the pressed flowers (see pressing techniques on pages 52-53) on the card, as desired. Carefully glue them into place with the soft art brush and with craft glue, using a toothpick to dab glue under the flowers as well as to gently remove the excess.

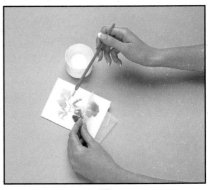

2. Mix an equal amount of water and white craft glue with the art brush. Brush it on the Sakuragami paper.

3. Seal the completed card with Sakuragami paper.

Materials:
2 pressed peonies
1 stem of pressed fern
1 stem of solidaster
tweezers
1 blank greeting card with matching envelope
soft art brush
water
white craft glue
toothpicks
Sakuragami paper
(to fit entire card)

Creating a framed floral composition can be fun and rewarding! Use your imagination to create a striking design suitable for any room in your house. Rounded flowers, tiny filler material, and greenery make the most pleasing arrangement. Keep larger, deeper-colored flowers near the base of the composition, allowing the finer materials to extend upward. Choose matte colors to accent the pressed flowers you are using.

1. On the piece of white art paper, use tweezers to arrange the pressed flowers (see pressing techniques on pages 52-53) in an upright pattern as they grow in nature. Carefully glue them into place with the soft art brush and white craft glue, using a toothpick to dab glue under the flowers as well as to gently remove the excess.

2. Place the double matte over the created scene.

3. Put the glass over the matted picture. Carefully insert it into the frame. Add backing and seal the back of the frame with the brown tape.

Materials:
9 × 12-inch piece of heavy white art paper

1 stem of pressed larkspur

3 stems of pressed Queen Anne's lace

4 stems of pressed solidaster

3 stems of pressed seafoam statice

2 stems of pressed dried clover

tweezers

white craft glue

soft art brush

toothpicks

double matte (green over pink) with a 5¼ × 8¼-inch opening

9 × 12-inch rectangular frame with glass

brown tape

Flowers under Glass

An artistic arrangement of pressed flowers creates a lasting keepsake, especially if the flowers used hold special meaning—a wonderful vacation, a memorable walk in the woods, a wedding. Remember that working in damp, humid weather can cause flowers to reabsorb moisture and lose their crispness and shape.

1. Using tweezers, arrange the pressed flowers (see pressing techniques on pages 52-53) on the white craft paper. Glue them into place using the soft art brush and white craft glue. Remove excess glue with a toothpick.

2. Place the double matte over the picture.

3. Put the glass over the matted picture. Carefully insert it into the frame. Add backing and seal the back of the frame with brown tape.

Materials

1 large pressed pansy	white craft glue
1 pressed buttercup	soft art brush
1 stem of maidenhair fern	toothpicks
assorted pressed greens	double matte (blue and yellow)
tweezers	with a 5 × 7-inch opening
9 × 12-inch sheet of white	9 × 12-inch oval frame with glass
art paper	brown tape

Romantic Floral Keepsake

Pretty as a Picture

Enhance your favorite photo with a matte embellished with lovely pressed flowers and greens. When selecting the materials, try to coordinate the color and varieties to the nature of the finished photo. Notice how well the blue matte is accented by the deep blue pansy, which in turn further coordinates with the floral bouquet being carried by the bride in the photo. Unity within the design will create a more pleasing appearance.

1. Carefully place the pressed flowers (see pressing techniques on pages 52-53) on the matte using tweezers. Glue them into place with the soft art brush and white craft glue when you are pleased with the placement. Remove excess glue with a toothpick.

2. Seal the entire placement with an equal mixture of craft glue and water using the soft art brush. Let it dry thoroughly. Place the decorated matte over the photograph.

3. Place the glass over the matted picture. Carefully insert it into the frame. Add backing and seal the back of the frame with brown tape.

Materials

double oval matte (yellow over blue) with a 5 × 7-inch opening

4 pressed pansies

5 pressed solidasters

3 pressed California poppies

2 stems of pressed evergreen

tweezers

white craft glue

water

soft art brush

tooth picks

5 × 7-inch oval photograph

9 × 12-inch oval frame with glass

brown tape

Resource List

Galerie Felix Flower
968 Lexington Avenue
New York, NY 10021
(212) 772-7701
(800) 359-7601

Galerie Felix Flower provides a wonderful selection of flowers and floral merchandise. Its line of merchandise includes silica gel for drying flowers, sprays to extend the life of dried flowers, flower presses, and containers. Galerie Felix Flower also carries how-to books and will provide instructions for creating dried flower arrangements. A catalog is available on request.

Rialto Florist Inc.
707 Lexington Avenue
New York, NY 10022
(800) 441-3234

Rialto Florist sells a complete array of dried flowers including flowers, pods, seeds, and thistles. Also in stock are types of soft foam used for making arrangements. If you have your heart set on a specific type of dried flower and cannot find it anywhere, you'll probably find it at Rialto Florist.

The Rosemary House
120 South Market Street
Mechanicsburg, PA 17055
(717) 697-5111

The Rosemary House carries an abundance of dried flowers, herbs, and spices. Also in stock are dried flower presses and wreaths made of dried flowers. The Rosemary House also carries packages of pressed flowers. A catalog is available on request.

Tom Thumb Workshops
Route 13, Box 357
Mappsville, VA 23407
(804) 824-3507
(800) 526-6502 (for orders only)

Tom Thumb Workshops offer a variety of dried flowers, wreaths, potpourri, herbs, spices, and fragrant oils. They also feature a craft newsletter and how-to magazines for people who want instructions on how to use what they buy. A catalog is available on request.

Also check local craft and variety stores: Pier 1 Imports Inc., Leewards Craft Bazaar, Frank's Nursery & Crafts, Inc., Michael's, and others in your area.